Shamanism

For Beginners! How to Understand and Implement a Shaman Way of Living

1st Edition

By Doc Mantles

© **Copyright 2018 by Doc Mantles. All rights reserved.**

This document is geared towards providing exact and reliable information in regards to the topic and issue covered. The publication is sold with the idea that the publisher is not required to render accounting, officially permitted, or otherwise, qualified services. If advice is necessary, legal or professional, a practiced individual in the profession should be ordered.

- From a Declaration of Principles which was accepted and approved equally by a Committee of the American Bar Association and a Committee of Publishers and Associations.

In no way is it legal to reproduce, duplicate, or transmit any part of this document in either electronic means or in printed format. Recording of this publication is strictly prohibited and any storage of this document is not allowed unless with written permission from the publisher. All rights reserved.

The information provided herein is stated to be truthful and consistent, in that any liability, in terms of inattention or otherwise, by any usage or abuse of any policies, processes, or directions contained within is the solitary and utter responsibility of the recipient reader. Under no circumstances will any legal responsibility or blame be held against the publisher for any reparation, damages, or monetary loss due to the information herein, either directly or indirectly.

Respective authors own all copyrights not held by the publisher.

The information herein is offered for informational purposes solely, and is universal as so. The presentation of the information is without contract or any type of guarantee assurance.

Table of Contents

Introduction 1
Chapter 1. Basics of Shamanism 3
What Shamans Believe 6
Uses of Shamanism 9
Shamans' Duties 10
The Source of the Shaman's Power 11
What Shamanism is NOT 11
How does a person become a Shaman? 13
Calling 16
Chapter 2. The Shamanic Reality 18
Chapter 3. Shamanic Skills 26
Finding the Right Shaman 28
Visualization 30
Awakening Your Psychic Abilities 32
Levels of Consciousness 35
Using Your Psychic Abilities 36
Being a Hollow Bone 38
Creating Sacred Space 40

- *Acquiring Protection* 40
- *Sticking to a Practice* 41
- Chapter 4. Shamanic Journeying 42
- *The 3 Worlds of the Shamanic Journey* 43
- I. Lower World 45
- II. Middle World 47
- III. Upper World 49
- *How to Enter the Upper World* 51
- How to Journey 51
- *Ending a Journey* 54
- *Shamanic Journey Precautions* 56
- *Grounding* 57
- *How to Ground Your Shamanic Journeys* 59
- Real Vs Imagined 59
- Chapter 5. Helping Spirits 61
- *Communicating With Spirit Guides* 62
- *Power Animals – What Are They?* 65
- *Finding Your Power Animal* 67
- Chapter 6. Shamanic Healing 69
- *Causes of Illnesses* 72

Chapter 7. Dreamwork 80

Chapter 8. Working with Plants 90

Ayahuasca 94

Plant Magic 97

Conclusion 102

Introduction

Shamanism existed way before religions and sciences dictated how people should live and what they should believe. Back then, almost all people on Earth had a shaman in their tribe; someone who served as the intermediary between humans and the divine spirits that dwelt in nature. A shaman is someone who is different from an ordinary human, thus he or she is given the responsibility to take care of others who don't possess the same powers that he/she does. Human life during these times were spent living in harmony with nature. The Earth provided for people, and in return, the people took care of it.

As time went on, people became more and more controlling of nature. They no longer believed in respecting other creatures since they could easily get what they wanted from them. Their greed came to a point that they have cleared vast tracts of land to make room for their houses and farms – later on, these turned into empires and cities, and in these places, the human population rapidly grew.

The walls that people have put around them are more than physical structures; they are also psychological and spiritual. Humans have forgotten their intimate connection with nature. They do not care about the environment for as long as they are secure in their artificial habitats.

Unfortunately, this illusion of security is gradually fading away; people are facing the consequences of their actions by experiencing calamities of scales never seen before.

You may have become interested in shamanism because of the powers that shamans possess, and you would like to have power yourself. You must know that shamans are chosen by the Spirit to serve others. Are you ready for the responsibility? Whatever you gain from shamanism is intended to help not only yourself, but others as well. This may be members of your own family, those in need, your community, or the world at large.

Are you willing to change yourself so you can return to the old ways? You may have lived a life that is designed for comfort and convenience. This includes having the belief that the only world that exists is this one that humans have dominated. By becoming a shaman, your eyes will be opened up into a universe vaster than you have ever known. This will make you humble, but at the same time, elevate your status, because you will recognize your connection with everything.

If you said yes to these questions, then you may be ready to become a shaman. Let us begin by getting familiar with what shamanism is and what it is not.

Chapter 1. Basics of Shamanism

Shamanism is basically the practice of shamans – individuals who can voluntarily enter altered states of consciousness to travel into otherworldly realms. It is a belief system but it is not a religion; there are no central authority figures that impose what is acceptable and what is heretical. There are no scriptures either (teachings were passed through word of mouth), thus there are no factions that disagree with one another when it comes to how sacred texts are to be interpreted.

It has existed for thousands of years in various lands – in Europe, Middle East, Central Asia, East Asia, South Asia, India, China, and so on. From what we have learned about our ancestors through artifacts and cave paintings, shamanism may have existed at least 30,000 years ago when humans were still hunter-gatherers.

Developments in human history changed our hunter-gathering ways, and this also affected shamanism. The invention of agriculture and the domestication of animals enabled man to conquer nature – this unsettled the shamanistic lifestyle of living in harmony with other living beings. The rise of various religions sought to eradicate beliefs that are different from what they teach by labeling them as lies from the devil. Technology further alienated people from nature and made people short-sighted and self-centered.

Science, although useful in a lot of ways, is presently unable to confirm shamanic realities, thus it contributes to people's disregard of shamanic beliefs. Thus, even though shamanism has been a crucial part of our ancestors' existence, it has dwindled greatly until only a few cultures practice it now.

Shamanism would have remained a secret among the few cultures that still practice it if not for the work of those who studied it and published books about it. The word "shamanism" itself was created by western explorers of Siberia during the 1600s. They used it to refer to the old religion of the Mongols, Turks, and those who speak the Tunguisic and Samoyedic languages in Northeast Asia, Eastern Siberia, and in the northernmost Eurasia. They converted the Tungus word samaan or s'amanthe, which meant "to know", into shaman, and they used it to refer to a leader of a Siberian tribe. When some anthropologists found similarities among practices in America, Africa, Asia, and Australasia, they also used shamanism to refer to them.

Knowledge from shamans came from archaeological or anthropological studies. Some researchers have lived with people who practice shamanism.

What Shamans Are

Shamans are considered as intermediaries for the human and spirit worlds. They travel to supernatural realms and communicate with spirits to gain information and energy that can help themselves and their communities. They can also do some things while in the spiritual worlds to create a desired result in this physical world.

People are considered as shamans only if they can enter an altered state of consciousness, journey to other worlds, and converse with spirits at will. Those who enter a trance or gets possessed by spirits without their control cannot be considered as shamans. Shamans are also grounded in reality and they make practical use of what they receive from their journeys. Although the insane may be in fact traversing other realities, they have lost touch with this reality, so they can't function as intermediaries.

Shamans need to be a stable bridge between this ordinary reality and others. This is why they need to be physically fit and psychologically stable. They have a heavy responsibility to their community since they serve as the leaders, advisers, protectors, and healers. This is why those who want to be shamans are often subjected to initiations that will test their limits.

What Shamans Believe

Animists believe that spirits exist everywhere. These spirits can be deities, nature spirits, or ghosts of the deceased or souls of the unborn. They could reside in objects and in the bodies of living beings such as humans and animals. They can cause illnesses and insanity, but they can also aid in healing and bestow wisdom. These spirits can also be responsible for the development of psychic powers. For animists, aside from individual spirits, there is a general spiritual energy that permeates the universe.

Shamans are animists, but not all animists are shamans. Shamans and animists believe that everything has a soul – that is, consciousness and life force – and everything is connected to one another in a deep level. What make shamans different from animists are their practices of journeying to spirit realms and interacting with spirits; animists just acknowledge their existence. Aside from that, animist priests invite spirits to enter our realm, but shamans go to the realms of the spirits.

Aside from believing that spirits are real, shamans acknowledge spirits' importance to the lives of individuals and to the society as a whole. They believe that these spirits can be malevolent or benevolent and have their own personalities, preferences, biases, and the like, so they have to be negotiated with. Sometimes, they must battle with spirits if they are causing harm or preventing something good from being attained.

Like regular people, shamans can be good or bad as well. They may choose to heal or choose to inflict harm. They may serve others or serve themselves. This is why some shamans do end up losing the favor of helping spirits if they use their powers for purposes that they don't approve of. Also, the interconnectedness of all things may cause them to experience the pain they've sent to another person.

Shamans see illnesses as caused, not only by physical factors, but spiritual and energetic elements as well. For them, these may be caused by malevolent energies and spirits, so they have to conquer the offending forces and repair the damages they've done. Their awareness may enter their patients' bodies to accomplish this.

Shamans perceive the energetic counterpart of physical things, emotions, and ideas. They often have extra-sensory perception and have a sharp intuition. They are adept at visualizing things – this is how they do their activities in the non-physical plane.

There is a shamanic belief that spirits in nature have agreed to help humans because we are young and in need of guidance. Thus, shamans often seek spirit guides and power animals that can help them with their missions.

The shaman's spirit is said to go out of the body when going to a different world, but people view this differently. Some say that his/her awareness expands to reach that destination, others say only a part of the soul goes out, while others claim that one of the shaman's many souls takes the journey. Regardless of what actually happens, the shaman experiences travelling and often returns with the things he/she has sought out for.

Shamans can perform divination to know the past, present, and future of something. They may use divinatory tools or consult the spirits to do this.

Shamans use plants in healing; they are experts in herbal medicine. They are more than just medicine men though because they can commune with the spirits of the plants. Sometimes, plant spirits teach them what to do to achieve certain goals and heal certain ailments.

Aside from plants, shamans use items that contain spirits. These may be naturally-occurring objects or created by the shaman.

Uses of Shamanism

There are people who are prejudiced against shamanism; they say that it is primitive and not necessary in modern society. On the contrary, a return to a shamanistic viewpoint may be what the society needs. Humanity has lost its old connection with nature thus many people are oblivious about the destruction we are causing to our home planet. Millions of plant and animal species have become extinct because of our own doing, and we now have weapons that can potentially wipe out large populations of people. Perhaps by seeing the world the way our shamanic ancestors do will help us regain our respect for our environment – and each other.

Aside from potentially saving ourselves from self-destruction, shamanism can help us in the level of communities and individuals. Shamanic practices can help heal not only the body, but also the emotions, the mind, and of course, the spirit. They are holistic compared to treatments that target only the body such as with medicinal procedures, or only the mind such as with psychological interventions, or the spirit such as with religious activities. Because a person is treated at multiple aspects, healing may be more complete and arrive more rapidly.

Shamans are also oriented towards the community. They can serve not only people within their own group, but they can also be peacekeepers between their group and others.

Because of their ability to see things from multiple perspectives, they can thoroughly understand the problems that arise between individuals and groups, and with their wisdom, solve them in the best ways possible.

Shamans' Duties

The duties of a shaman vary among cultures and circumstances.

In general, they serve as intermediaries or messengers between the human world and the spiritual worlds. They serve as healers by treating illnesses and ailments not only through medicine that target the body, but also by mending the person's soul. They mediate between the tribe's inner life and its external activities. They preside over rites of passages, marriages, and deaths. They help the dying cross over to the next world by serving as psychopomps. They perform rituals for themselves, for certain individuals, for their own families, and for their entire community or tribe. In times of crisis such as natural disasters or conflict, they can seek help and protection from the forces of nature.

Shamans can also serve as the keepers of knowledge of the tribe. They have a wide knowledge of the tribe's history, beliefs, myths, lineage, healing practices, and the like.

During ancient times, shamans help with the success of hunts. They did this by releasing animal souls from their abodes. They also teach hunters how to behave towards those they hunt so they don't feel hurt or angry and tell the living others to avoid the hunters. They help infertile women to bear children by obtaining the soul of her future child.

The Source of the Shaman's Power

The shaman's power doesn't come from his/her own human abilities but from the spirits. He/she must only be good in hollowing himself/herself to serve as an effective conduit for the spirits' influence.

To achieve this task, the shaman must master the ability to enter trances, to have visions, and to control his/her dreams.

What Shamanism is NOT

Religions may practice shamanism, but shamanism itself is not considered as a religion. It is a set of beliefs, traditions, and practices that may vary between groups. As an example, shamanism in Korea is influenced by Buddhism and Taoism.

Shamanism is not a simple form of therapy; it is a way of life. Shamans believe in certain things and they act in accordance to those beliefs. Becoming a shaman is not easy, so they do their best in carrying out their duties since not everyone can be a shaman like them.

Being a shaman is not simply being a nature lover. Simply being appreciative of nature does make person become aware of the sentient forces underlying nature. A person who spends time in beautiful environments may find his/her awareness wandering, but this is unlike the intentional journeying of the shamans.

It is not merely entertainment. It involves hard work and responsibility. Shamanistic practices were created out of genuine need. Back then, people relied on shamans for diverse needs such as healing, protection, counseling, and resolving conflicts. Shamans are responsible for appeasing spirits so that the tribe would be spared from harm. They call on the spirits of animals and plants so that the tribe will have something to eat. Even if other things have replaced the shaman's services, these shamans still have big responsibilities towards their fellow human beings.

Modern times separated humans from nature and the spiritual so they don't have to rely on intermediaries that much. Nowadays, people turn to shamanism for recreation or self-help. This is not bad, but there is a tendency for shamanism to be purposed for impractical reasons. To counteract this, it's important for you to apply whatever you gain from shamanic experiences into your daily life. Your shamanic activities must help you or someone else like they were meant to do.

How does a person become a Shaman?

Traditionally, shamans are part of an indigenous community. They are respected by the tribe they belong to since they serve as the intermediaries to the divine. Before becoming shamans, they are usually trained by teachers and tested before they become accepted for the role.

There is a widespread belief that shamans are chosen by the spirits. As they grow up, doing what shamans do become natural for them. They see spirits easily and talk to them as they would a normal person.

The Evenk believe that the spirits choose the souls who will be shamans. According to their belief, before babies are born, their souls sit on the branches of the World Tree. In fact, they believe that everyone sits on these branches, but those who are destined to be shamans are given their own. They say that if the spirits chose one to be a shaman, there is nothing that he/she could do about it. And if someone is not chosen, there is also nothing he/she could do to change it.

Being a shaman is a heavy responsibility, and the spirits can be demanding. It is said that those who were chosen to be shamans but refused to be one may become ill to the point of death.

Shamans may be taught. In general, shamans are taught by the spirits. Human teachers may find and teach apprentices, but the most they can do is introduce their apprentice to the guiding spirits.

There is also a belief that the Great Spirit itself can decide to incarnate as a human shaman. When this happens, it becomes known by the elders of the tribe. They know when the Spirit will incarnate and in whose body it will incarnate in.

The shaman role is also often passed down through the generations. Young apprentices are also guided by elders. Those who are interested in becoming shamans are also initiated. This initiation involves different tests, and those who are able to withstand the challenges and demonstrate their prowess become shamans.

In more traditional communities, the shamans or the elders choose who will become shamans in their tribe. The way they do this depends on the culture, though. Some accept only those who have a lineage. Some select those who are close with the spirits ever since they are children. Individuals who may be prone to spirit contacts may become shamans after being trained. These are the people who enter involuntary trances and get possessed often.

People who are prone to trances, out of body experiences, and vivid dreams may also be considered. Through these experiences, they are thought to have been initiated by the spirits into shamanism.

People may have a calling to become shamans. They may develop an illness or have a Near Death Experience where they become visited by ancestors, ghosts, or spirits who invite them to the shamanistic path. Those who have died and come back may eventually become shamans since they have known death and have reached the realms that only spirits can reach.

Would-be shamans are often led by signs around them or in dreams. It is said that fate also brings them to those who can teach them how to become shamans, or to have experiences that will teach them how to be one. They may have a physical illness or a psychological crisis that develop their abilities to perceive the shamanic reality and heal others. They may understand others' sickness and how to heal it by becoming ill themselves.

Initiations often include the theme of death and resurrection. They undergo grueling experiences that may involve fasting or the ingestion of drugs. Some may lie on bed immobilized for up to a week and experience a series of realistic dreams.

You can be a shaman when you become accepted by a tribe. After this, you must respect and follow the culture's spirituality under the guidance of the leaders and with responsibility for what you're doing. You must also support the group with its struggles.

Some believe that lightning represents divine mystical energy. Those who get struck by lightning can be considered as chosen by the gods to become a shaman.

Calling

If you feel incredibly to shamanism, you might be receiving "the call". Below are some of the characteristics that may have led to this:

- You have experienced or often experience unexplainable things
- You had a Near Death Experience
- You had an Out of Body Experience
- You have been present for numerous deaths or births
- People often go to you to seek advice
- People find it easy to reveal their secrets to you
- You find comfort and regain your strength in nature
- You have empathic abilities – it's easy for you to feel others' emotions
- You are a mind-reader

- You have memories of past lives as a shaman, seer, or healer
- You are good in solving things using your intuition
- You are highly creative
- You can willfully control the dreams you have
- You can see spirits and subtle energies
- You can communicate with animals and plants

These are just some signs of having a calling towards shamanism. The fact that you are reading this book is already proof of it.

Now that you are acquainted with the basics of shamanism, it is time for you to learn about the Shamanic Reality, the place familiar to all shamans.

Chapter 2. The Shamanic Reality

We live in a reality that is composed of physical, tangible objects and non-physical ideas, concepts, and emotions. What is commonly thought of as real is what we can agree on existing – these are things we can perceive with our five senses or register with technological devices. They are usually objects that exist outside of us, and if they no longer exist, they have left some evidence of their previous existence. However, there are things that we can't see, touch, or hear - such as the emotion of love or the concept of freedom – but these are still real because we can understand it, we experience it, or we have seen examples of it in our lives. In short, we can say that something is real if different people have somewhat consistent experiences of it.

The Shamanic Reality is a reality that not everyone can perceive all the time, but those who enter an altered state of consciousness may witness it. Those who have studied shamanism among different cultures from different parts of the globe have noticed similarities in beliefs, practices, and experiences. When there are differences, they almost always shallow, and shamans from opposite sides of the globe can talk to one another and understand what each one is saying.

Those who take on shamanic journeys, even those who are new to it and have no expectations of what will happen, experience similar things and are taught similar lessons. Just as with ordinary reality, this consistency serves as proof that the shamanic reality exists.

People may experience variations, but these are superficial. For example, a Christian who travels to the Upper World may see visions of Jesus Christ and the angels, a Muslim may perceive Allah and Mohammed, a Wiccan may see the triple goddess in the form of the Mother, the Maiden, and the Crone. Pet lovers who journey to the lower world may meet their deceased pets; zookeepers may encounter wild animals, while those who like myths may find mythological creatures. Although each of these people witness different things, they belong to the same themes.

Reality to us is something that is formed by our brains. Light and sounds exists as waves, but to us, light appears as brightness and colors, while sounds have volume and tones. We don't have any objective measurements of what non-physical realities are – they can be energies, frequencies, thought forms or something we have no idea about – but our minds translate them into something we can work with. Thus, the Upper World contains deities, and they will be seen in the forms that the person is ready to see, and the Lower World have animals, and likewise, they will show themselves in forms that are familiar to the viewer.

As mentioned earlier, for shamans, everything has a soul and this includes living beings, land formations, celestial objects. Aside from these, ceremonies and ritual objects likewise possess a soul. Concepts, emotions, events, places, and illnesses likewise have souls. Since souls are composed of consciousness and life energies, this means that they may be communicated with.

Shamans can shapeshift or transform themselves to identify with something else – spirits, animals, even diseases.

The Shamanic Reality is an example of non-ordinary reality. Normal people access non-ordinary reality at some point. It is described to be an invisible world where spirits, the saints, and God is. It is where everything is already known, and everything that will happen has already occurred.

When people glimpse this reality, they label it as fantasies or psychosis. Sometimes the just shrug it off and are content to label it as something they can't explain Unlike the insane, the shaman knows how to move to these parallel realities, do things while in it, and bring back useful things to normal life.

States of Consciousness

Altered States of Consciousness: The shaman can achieve what he/she does by entering an altered state of consciousness. This means entering a state of mind that's different from the normal. The normal state of consciousness keeps us anchored in ordinary reality; it is what we use when we do normal stuff like work, do chores, socialize, and so on.

Normal Altered States: We normally enter an altered state of consciousness at certain times of the day and while doing certain activities. The moments just right before waking up and immediately before falling asleep are times when we are in a light trance. You may have noticed hallucinations during these periods. Dreaming is another form of an altered state since you are aware but you are in a mental realm. Meditation and prayer involves focusing your attention inwards and away from external stimuli – this is a form of trance as well.

Reaching Different States of Consciousness

- *Relaxation*

Relaxing deeply changes your brainwaves and enables you to tune in to subtle signals that get filtered out when you are in your normal awareness.

- ***Focused attention***

Being immersed in something such as an activity, an artwork, music, or beautiful scenery causes changes in your mental state. Meditating upon something or participating in a ritual also achieves this effect.

- ***Abnormal Conditions***

Sensory deprivation causes hallucinations as the brain turns its attention to inner senses. Being sleep deprived, overly stressed or extremely sick can disrupt the normal functioning of the brain and cause hallucinations as well.

- ***Mind-Altering Substances***

Taking mind-altering substances such as hallucinogens and entheogens (hallucination-inducing plants) are sometimes done by shamans and other people to explore other realities. Not all shamans do this but it can help with their shamanic works.

- ***Breathwork***

Many religions and mystical traditions associate our breaths with the spirit. Certain breathing techniques will help achieve certain effects, including an altered consciousness.

- *Movement*

Spinning, twirling, and dancing is known to help propel a person into an altered state. This can be seen in many old rituals where those participating dance themselves into a trance. However, you need not do that in order to achieve the same thing; sometimes, doing something simple (such as household chores) with focused attention can work.

- *Aromas*

Smells can have effects on a person's mental state – for example, lavender is calming while citrus is invigorating. Perfumes, incense, oils, and the like can be used to put a person in the desired state of mind.

- *Journeys to sacred sites*

The act of journeying puts one in a meditative state of mind. The place itself may also contain energies that help induce trance.

- *Purification*

Purification rituals such as fasting, pushing one's limits, or tormenting one's self may trigger an altered state of mind.

- *Drumming*

Drumming serves an important part in shamanic journeying. It brings the shaman into a state of mind that is conducive for travelling. It also guides his/her travel and signals when the journey is almost over.

Drums in shamanism are played between 200 – 240 beats per minute, or around 4 beats per second or less. This rhythm is said to affect the brain in such a way that a few minutes of drumming produces theta brainwaves that are witnessed in hours of deep meditation. Aside from the speed, the drums are tuned to produce rich undertones and overtones. The brain can't process these sounds well, so it becomes prone to creating stuff to make sense of what is heard. As a result, auditory hallucinations such as singing, whistling, bird song, chanting, and all sorts of sounds may be heard. In certain individuals, drumming may activate synaesthesia or the crossover of senses – sounds can be seen as images or felt as sensations, scents, or tastes.

Signs of Altered State of Consciousness

Some signs that you are in an altered state of mind are hallucinations (you can see things or hear sounds that are not from the physical environment) and the internal dialogue is subdued or is completely silent.

There are some easy ways to enter an altered state:

- Relaxing physically by assuming the most comfortable position possible and releasing muscle tension

- Relaxing mentally by letting go of concerns and thinking about thoughts that make you feel calm

- Reducing sensory stimuli by closing your eyes or wearing a blindfold, dimming or switching off the lights, turning off the TV and radio, putting away your phone, etc.

- Keeping as still as possible without straining

- Breathing calmly and deeply

The Shamanic Reality is entered through an altered state of consciousness. The next chapter is about crucial skills that a shaman must possess to be able to function in this reality.

Chapter 3. Shamanic Skills

The best way to become a shaman is to become an apprentice under one. Those who are born into shamanic families are often raised to become shamans. They will be taught by their relatives or by the teachers in their group.

If you don't belong to such as family or tribe, you will have to seek your own teacher. It's fortunate that shamanism has regained its popularity in modern times so you can easily search for shamanism workshops online. You may event opt take an online course or participate in a class in person.

You could learn on your own, of course, but this involves trial and error. Having experienced guides will make you progress faster since you will be taught the proper way of doing things and how to avoid mistakes. Learning on your own will be cheaper and you could do it at your own pace, though.

Be warned that simply reading a book or attending one workshop will not turn you into a shaman outright. It takes a long time to learn and master shamanic skills, and so much more to be considered as an authentic shaman. Some train their entire lives, constantly learning and relearning.

<u>Shamanism is not a hobby or a way to acquire fame or riches.</u> It requires commitment to establish connections with the spirit and to serve one's community. Those who want to be shamans are often tested through initiations and events in their lives. Only those who pass the trials successfully gain the power that they seek, and this power is not to be used for selfish ends but in service.

The Training Process

Shamanic training is often held in remote natural settings. The trainees are isolated from common preoccupations such as their families, work, technology, leisurely activities and the like. This is done so they can fully focus on the training.

The apprentices may be tasked to follow a strict routine, which includes consuming only prescribed food and drink. They are also often told to do certain practices like meditation, rituals, and exercises for prolonged periods of time. Initiations may involve conversing with spirits and undergoing trials to prove one's worth.

Learning about plants will also involve going to places where they can be found and experimenting with them. Some teachers let their students eat a part of the plant so they can be familiar with it.

Finding the Right Shaman

There was a time when word about shamans were spread through word of mouth. Their stories, sometimes turning into stuff of legend. In this time and age, many shamans are freely advertising their services to serve more people. You could find their blogs and ads online.

Although it's easier to find shamans nowadays, it may be a bit harder to find someone you can actually trust. Back then, shamans become known because of how well they do, but the internet and media in general has made it easier for people to pretend to be someone they're not.

Before choosing a shaman to help you, you must check their background first. Is this person involved with any crime or scandal? Can you get feedback from this shaman's previous clients? What is he/she known for? What is his/her personality? How does he/she treat people?

<u>Keep the following in mind:</u>

- Learn more about the shaman's methods and specialties. What are the things he/she does? Are the activities done in a group setting or on a one-on-one basis?

- There are shamans who specialize in certain things like curing illnesses, breaking addictions, treating phobias, restoring energetic balance, retrieving soul fragments, and the like

- The shaman you choose will depend on your preferences. Some shamans teach while others don't; you must ask them if they are willing to teach you and what they require for it.

- Consider the shaman's qualities. He/she must be someone who is genuinely trustworthy. Don't trust someone just because he/she tells you to, even if that person claims to be powerful.

- Real shamans may have real power, but they don't let it inflate their egos. They deeply understand that their own pride will get in the way of perceiving reality and interacting with the spirit world effectively. They don't push other people's boundaries but maintain respect. They are accepting of people despite their flaws.

- They don't force you to hire them; they let you come to them when you want to. They have a peaceful aura.

- They must be transparent. Ask them how they became a shaman. They should be capable of telling you an authentic story of how they turned into one. If they became defensive or if you noticed inconsistencies in what they say, you may be talking to a fraud.

- Most importantly, you must listen to your intuition. If something about the shaman bothers you, don't pursue him/her anymore. There may be other teachers and shamans who will be a better match for you.

Visualization

Shamanic tasks require a lot of visualizations, so you must get used to picturing things in your mind. It's good if you normally think in pictures or daydream a lot; if not, you must exercise your imagination more.

- <u>Visualization Exercise 1</u>

Get an illustrated story book and spend time looking at the pictures. Recall your experiences as a child when your parents read you fairy tales. You may remember not only hearing the words but also the pictures and emotions that played in your awareness. Relive these kinds of moments as you read fiction.

- <u>Visualization Exercise 2</u>

Get a pen and paper then draw the letters I and Y next to each other. Look at the Y for a few moments then cover it with one hand. Move your eyes toward the letter I and imagine it splitting in the middle to become the letter Y. Visualize one of the arms growing longer than the other one. Do the same with the other arm.

- <u>Visualization Exercise 3</u>

Make it a habit to close your eyes and visualize everyday objects, such as your phone, your watch, your car, and so on. See them in your mind in as much detail as possible. You may look at them first before seeing them in your mind or recreate their images purely from memory.

- <u>Visualization Exercise 4</u>

When you are in a busy place where there are many people, watch them as they do their business. When some people pass you by, look at them and keep their image in your head. Imagine where they could be going and what they could be doing later on. Observe what else you will see in your mind.

- <u>Visualization Exercise 5</u>

Choose a drawing, painting, or photograph that you like. It's better if the picture is not bothersome and simple. Be in a quiet place where you can stay for a few minutes without being distracted. Sit in a comfortable position and take deep breaths so you can relax. Gaze at the picture for a few minutes while tuning out other thoughts. Try to remember every detail.

When you feel ready, close your eyes and recall the picture. Describe it in your mind. Try to see the pictures in both images and words. Open your eyes and look at the picture. What did you remember correctly? What did you miss out? Close your eyes again and imagine that you're merging with the picture. Look around you, take a walk in your new environment, and interact with the things and creatures you encounter.

Awakening Your Psychic Abilities

Some people are born with strong psychic senses, but not everyone really nurtures them. However, they could be developed by anyone through practice. If you want to be a shaman, you must exercise your psychic side so that you can perceive the worlds where the spirits are.

Before you can hone your psychic senses, you must use more of your normal senses first. This is because psychic information may be translated into a sensory impression – a vision, a sound, a sensation – in your mind. If you habitually ignore what your five senses pick up, it's also likely that you will ignore what your sixth sense picks up.

Take this moment to pay more attention to what is going on around you. Look around. What can you see around you? Do things look the way they expect them to be, or are there any unusual sights? Are you seeing things that you don't usually see because you are preoccupied with something else? Pick an object that interests you. Can you tell what material it is made of based on its appearance? How would it feel like if you touched it? Would it make a sound if you strike it? What could it taste like if it has become edible?

What are you hearing? You may have tuned out the sounds of the traffic or the fan because you have grown used to them. Listen to them again. Are they making loud or soft noises? Can you pick up a melody from them? Are there any sounds you can hear that you can't see the source of? What could possibly be making those noises? If you hear human voices, can you guess whether a child or an adult is making them? Are they male or female? What is their personality like?

Feel the breeze on your skin. What is the weather like? How cold is the air compared to your body warmth? How do your clothes feel? Explore the ground with your feet. Without looking, can you tell whether you are standing on cement, hardwood floor, soil, or sand? Of course you have seen the floor before and you know by sight what it is, but can you arrive to the same conclusion if you don't use your eyes?

Pretend that you are a child again. Everything is new to you so everything is fascinating. You don't know what this and that is so you don't have any judgments of them. By noticing fully and not shielding your perception with preoccupations and internal dialogue, you will get more input from both your normal senses and your psychic senses.

Make the most of your senses and extend them to the realm beyond the senses. The exercises above first focused on the things you can actually sense, but later on it went into guessing things that are not accessible to you at the moment. Try this with different things and check whether you guessed correctly. The more you do this, the more you will be able to find indications as to whether you are receiving genuine psychic information or making up things based on your preconceptions. It takes a lot of trial and error, but when you get the hang of it, it'll be worth it.

Awakening your psychic ability is something you do with your mind. This is because there are worlds that are beyond the senses but are accessible through the mind. With your mind, you can go to the past and the future, be somewhere far away, and create things and environments out of thin air. The power of your mind allows you to create and explore worlds.

Sure, your mind can create fantasies that can be easily disregarded because they are not real. However, your mind also has the ability to explore unseen realms that are real in the sense that they could also be perceived and interacted with by other people. You will learn more about these kinds of realms later on.

You must develop your "shamanic eyes" or a new way of perceiving things by using more of your senses and imagination. You must be willing to accept that imagined things may be real at some level. You will become more shaman-like this way.

Levels of Consciousness

It will become easier to notice and train your psychic powers if you understand where psychic information comes from: your subconscious mind. There are three levels of consciousness that are involved in psychic development: the conscious mind, the subconscious mind, and the superconscious mind. These three balance the messages they receive from each other to keep you safe and sane.

Your conscious mind is responsible for reasoning, analysis, and decision-making. To be efficient, it maintains objectivity and filters out information so it can focus on what it considers as important.

The subconscious mind is like a computer that takes in information that slips past the conscious mind's attention. It will become overwhelming for the conscious mind to process every single detail of what you experience so the subconscious just stores these way like books in a library. However, if the subconscious mind is activated by necessity, meditative exercises, psychoactive substances, or relaxation, it can release helpful data back to the conscious mind.

Although the subconscious mind is powerful in itself, it is just a part of a more powerful and wiser mind – the superconscious mind. This is considered as the universal mind where instincts, insights, psychic signals, and spiritual wisdom come from. Although your subconscious mind is storage for your own personal experiences and issues, it also serves as the bridge between your individual consciousness and that of everyone and everything else's. Some consider this as the collective consciousness or the Akashic Records.

You can tap into your subconscious mind by building your imagination and controlling your thoughts. You must stop being engrossed with your conscious mind's preoccupations, silence your internal dialogues, and simply listen to what else you can perceive.

Using Your Psychic Abilities

Psychic abilities could involve visions (clairvoyance), sounds (clairaudience), sensations (clairsentience), smells (clairalience), and tastes (clairgustance). It can also come in the form of emotions (empathy) and thoughts (telepathy). Sometimes you may just have a knowing about something; this can be considered as intuitive insights.

Using psychic abilities requires clearing your mind as much as possible. Anything that remains in your awareness may influence whatever you will perceive. If you are afraid of something, for example, you may see scary spirits around you. Give yourself 5 to 10 minutes to empty out your mind.

When you have reached an altered state of consciousness, focus on a target you want to know more of, or ask your question. Without thinking of anything else, wait for the response. Your subconscious mind's reply may come in the form of visions memories, symbols, ideas, sounds, and others.

It is possible that your imagination will make up things according to your preoccupations, expectations, preferences, biases, worries, and wishes. This is why it is important to be calm, non-judging, and unattached to results. If you can't perceive anything, don't force it to happen but instead slide deeper into relaxation. You might be getting a blank because a part of your conscious mind is fighting off the psychic signals; the more you relax, the more your conscious mind will release its control over your awareness.

Try to record whatever enters your mind. You can do this by speaking into a recorder or jotting down notes. Simply gather information without analyzing them for the meantime.

When the stream of information is slowing down or if you catch yourself forcing what you perceive, stop recording.

You will discover that psychic impressions may be straightforward and literal, but other times they may also be symbolic and vague. When you have collected the psychic data, you can switch back to the reasoning, analytical mode of the conscious mind. This time, you will decipher your psychic impressions. Try to interpret them even if you're unsure about their meaning. Later on, collect information about the target or find the answers to your question. Check where you got it right and where you made mistakes.

Eventually, you will find some patterns that will help you know the meaning of specific psychic signals. For instance, you may learn that your subconscious mind's "word" for good news is vision of a feather and bad news as a boulder. From these, you can create a psychic dictionary that helps you reliably interpret psychic signals.

Being a Hollow Bone

The power of the shaman doesn't belong to him/her. He/she only acts as a form of a "hollow bone" that allows the powers of the spirit to come through and manifest in our reality. This is why being empty is crucial in being an effective shaman.

The ego is the false self that creates a make-believe world, an illusory one that makes living a bit more predictable and more convenient. It is composed of who you think you are and how you define yourself, and your beliefs of how the world should be. The things that prevent you from acquiring psychic information such as fears, biases, and expectations are products of this ego. These beliefs and narratives may prevent you from doing what shamans do.

This false world is reinforced by accepting it without question and telling it to others. Sometimes when this view is threatened, we react with hostility and refuse to acknowledge different viewpoints. To perceive the shamanic reality, you must refrain from upholding this false world and false self.

Who you think you are is just a construction; there is a real self that experiences your experiences but are not attached to them. Be more aware of the self that is watching the experiences instead of simply experiencing things and associating yourself with them. Become the unrestrained awareness that can travel to different worlds.

The more that you can hollow yourself out, the more authentic your experiences will become. If you failed to empty yourself, what you will perceive will be filtered and distorted by your own prejudices, expectations, biases, and so on. You have to step away from these, but you may return to them after the journey. This process takes practice, but the more that you do this, the easier it will become.

Creating Sacred Space

A sacred space is the place in the physical world where you can perform your shamanic exercises. Many traditions prescribe their own guidelines about how a sacred space should look like; you may choose a tradition and follow its guidelines or just find a space where you feel inspired, comfortable, and safe. What's important is that it will effectively serve its purpose as a place that links the physical and spiritual dimensions.

This place should be somewhere you can carry out your activities in peace. It's better if there is nothing distracting around.

This place must have objects that are necessary for your work or are special to you. Don't clutter the space with unnecessary items.

Use dim lights or candles. Don't use overly bright lights because they may prevent you from entering trance.

If you want, play comforting sounds such as nature sounds, gentle music.

Acquiring Protection

Shamans call on protector spirits for their travels and other activities. They can request their presence when they are performing rituals, especially if they are fighting against an attack or curing an illness that has a predatory spirit.

Shaman armor may be worn – this is ritual clothing that has empowered objects that contain beneficial energies and helpful spirits.

Mirrors may be used to deflect harm and attacks sent the shaman's way. Aside from this, you may use any item that symbolizes protection for you.

Sticking to a Practice

Shamanism has a lot of potential so it has survived for a long time. It has also diversified enough that there are literally thousands of practices to choose from. However, you must avoid the temptation of switching from one practice to another without fully mastering any. It is by practicing and working deeply in the invisible realms that enable the shaman to tap into powers that create healing and change.

These are the essential skills for shamanic work. The following chapter is about shamanic journeying to the realms where the work is done.

Chapter 4. Shamanic Journeying

A shamanic journey involves moving away from ordinary reality to shamanic reality to contact spirits, acquire or recover energy, or gather information. It is often done with drumbeats playing in the background. Many cultures believe that the sound of the drums help the shaman enter an altered state of awareness and carry his/her soul towards where he/she wants to be.

Some even see the drumbeats as cords that connect to the listeners and transport them to other realms – the Australian aborigines called this the Dreamtime, the Celts label this as "the other world", while some consider them as parallel universes.

In some rituals, the drums are accompanied with rattles and other musical instruments. Shamanic songs called Icaros may be sung as well.

Embarking on a shamanic journey requires entering a trance, preferably that where Theta brainwaves are predominant. You will recognize this as a state between wakefulness and sleep.

Plant medicines may be used for more potent effects. Shamans learn what plans to use from previous shamans or from the spirits of the plants themselves. They believe that certain plants have powerful spiritual entities within them – as an example, they call ayahuasca as "mother ayahuasca". Aside from it, Peyote, Salvia, Magic Mushrooms, the San Pedro cactus, and Iboga may be used.

The 3 Worlds of the Shamanic Journey

For the Shaman, there are three worlds that are connected to each other and are equal to each other. These worlds form the mythological *World Tree* that is believed in almost all cultures. The <u>Lower World</u> forms the roots of this tree, the <u>Middle World</u> is its trunk, and the <u>Upper World</u> is its branches. This is believed to be the center of the universe, thus it is also called the axis mundi or the world axis.

Although the image of a tree can give you an idea that the Lower and Upper Worlds do not meet, they are actually connected. It is said that if you ascend further and further up the Upper World, you will find yourself in the Lower World, and if you descend deeper and deeper into the Lower World, you will end up in the Upper World.

Potentially all people can travel the axis mundi because it exists within each of our souls. The worlds that it connects are essentially inner planes of consciousness. Although the experiences and activities within these worlds do not take place at a physical level, they are not unreal. Humans didn't create these worlds; they discovered and then explored them.

It's possible that these worlds are within the collective unconscious of humanity. This is something that we humans are all connected to, and it is part of our minds whether we become conscious of it or not.

Each world contains unique qualities, thus, the kind of things that may be obtained from each world may differ from one another. The inhabitants and sights of this world also have their own peculiarities. Each realm requires a particular set of skills and quality of awareness from the traveler.

It is important to recognize the distinguishing characteristics of each realm to know where you are. You also need to know how to move between the worlds at will.

The axis mundi is where the three worlds connect; it is where the veils that separate our world and the shamanic worlds are thinner so it becomes easier to move across the worlds. The axis mundi is mythological, but there are representations of it in this world. After all, the axis mundi connects the different worlds together so you could find it in the actual world as well. Look for places in nature that has an otherworldly quality to it. You must feel peaceful in this area.

Go to this place physically or in your mind. Look at the surrounding with shamanic eyes or with the eyes of your mind. Have the intention of accessing the shamanic worlds through this place.

I. Lower World

The Lower World is often confused with hell, but you won't find flames, monsters, or demons in here. Far from being a place of torment, this world is where the replenishing energies of nature dwell. In here, you can commune and connect with aspects of nature – spirits of natural land and water formations, the elements of water, fire, air, earth, plant and animal life, to name a few things.

You can gain wisdom from animal and plant spirits in this world. They can bestow good qualities upon you – the swiftness of the cheetah or the strength of a bear, for example. Plants can teach you about healing. You may be taught like a student or you may experiment by interacting with the plants you find in there; you may consume them if you wish and observe their effects.

Since it also deals with "roots" you can seek counsel from your ancestors and take part in your tribal heritage here. The spirits of the dead sometimes end up here. Shamans who are looking for wandering souls go here to check.

In terms of the psyche, the Lower World corresponds to the Subconscious Mind. It deals with habits, instincts, deep emotions, and dreams. There are challenges and tests at this dimension, but there are also helping spirits that can help you overcome them.

Those who journey towards this realm have described this to be an earthy, natural environment such as a jungle, forest, cave, or river. If there are people in there, they appear to be cavemen or indigenous tribes. There are often no signs of technology around. There are also plenty of animals roaming freely.

How to Enter the Lower World

The Lower World can be entered by visualizing a scene found in nature.

- Find an entry point that goes into the earth. This may be a cave, an animal burrow, a volcano, a hole in the ground such as a manhole, through a hollow tree or log, or by diving into a pool of water.

- If you're more comfortable using familiar modes of transportation, you may imagine riding a descending elevator or escalator. You can also visualize walking down a staircase or sliding down an incline.

II. Middle World

The Middle World is the non-physical dimension of the world we live in. This is where our waking reality is located, and where we use ordinary consciousness in.

This world is accessed to gain answers to different worldly problems such as financial issues or relationship problems. Since this place is the energetic counterpart of our physical reality, shamans go here to find missing objects and people. Remotely viewing locations and people is done here. Shamans may also attempt to communicate with or influence people in this dimension.

Those who want to experience nature in its pure energy form may go to the Middle World. Take note that Nature here is different from the Lower World – in the Lower World, Nature exists in raw form and the creatures are the Oversouls or archetypes of individual creatures. It is the source of the energy of nature so it is more potent. In the Middle World, the nature essence is from the physical reality, so it emanates from existing living beings and natural formations. When people go to this world, they may acquire a deeper respect and appreciation for their natural environment, and likewise gain a better understanding of nature.

Shamans who are seeking cures from the physical world visit this place to seek out what they need. Those who are hunting game or looking for special kinds of plants go to this world.

It is said that the Middle World is the most chaotic of the three worlds. This is also where most of the confused spirits are found. These are the souls of the deceased who don't realize that they are dead already or those who refuse to leave the world they are used to. Because of their issues, they may cause problems to the traveler, and many travelers choose not to go into the Middle World.

Those who are travelling out of their bodies first find themselves here. The spirits of the deceased also linger here before they move on to other planes of existence. Thus, if people are having problems with hauntings, the Shaman negotiates with the lost souls that are causing the effects in the place. These shamans will serve as psychopomps that guide them to where they should be going.

Since the Middle World is the one which is most similar to our world, its inhabitants are a mixed variety. Some are kind-hearted and helpful while others are cruel and mischievous. You may find helping spirits here and they are the ones who would provide the most practical advice, but you have to guard against trickster spirits.

Aside from individual characters and creatures, you will find here the energetic forms of beliefs, thoughts, intentions, and emotions. Subtle energies will manifest themselves here as well. This will allow you to read the aura of people, objects, or places.

In the psyche, the Middle World is *represented by the conscious mind or Ego.*

III. Upper World

The Upper World can be thought of as Heaven – and indeed, deities and angels may be found in this place – but it is not exactly like it. It is in fact the realm of the cosmos, where the stars are. It is the realm of archetypes, of blueprints, and potentials that guide how reality manifests itself. Whatever exists in the physical plane is said to be a shadow of something that exists in the Upper World.

Spirit travelers describe this dimension as being abstract and ethereal. It is illuminated by pastel-colored light. Intricately designed temples, castles, and buildings may be found here, but again, there is usually know sign of modern technology as these are found in the Middle World.

You may find angels in here, as well as saints, holy people, archetypes, planetary beings, and dwellers of the cosmos. Deities may be found roaming around here, but the Ultimate Deity, the Creator and Source of all is found in all Three Worlds.

Although animals are more common in the Lower and Middle Worlds, they may be encountered in the Upper World as well but in mythological forms. The higher consciousness, the higher self, or superconscious mind of man finds its place here in this Word.

Shamans travel to this world to obtain knowledge of archetypes, to lead a vision into manifestation, or to guide events in the physical world. Interacting with archetypes in this realm enables the Shaman to interact with their physical counterparts. They also go there to receive inspiration and insights on how to restore balance between nature, humans, and the divine.

Questions that are usually asked here do not belong to practical, worldly concerns but are more philosophical and spiritual. You can ask about what decision is for the greater good of people or seek guidance regarding your true purpose in life.

Since the blueprints of the Universe and of life are here, you may want to go here if you intend to learn more about the laws of the cosmos and the secrets of life.

Conversing with deities and holy people is best done here.

The deceased may be found in here as well, including departed pets.

How to Enter the Upper World

The Upper World may be reached by imagining that you're climbing a tree or ladder that reach the sky. You may also visualize yourself to be in a high place such as a mountaintop or skyscraper. To climb up, you can travel by escalator or elevator, or see yourself as being carried up on smoke, on a magic carpet, a rocket, a balloon, a large bird or a flock of birds, or anything that ascends. You may pretend to be cloud or mist that rises until you enter the Upper World. You can also fly or float upwards.

You can enter the Upper World through a gap in the clouds, such as where sunlight shines through.

How to Journey

Journeying is commonly done lying down with the eyes closed, but it can also be done while standing, sitting, walking, singing, chanting, dancing. To leave the physical Middle World and go to the other worlds, you must put yourself in an altered state of consciousness and maintain this for the duration of your travel. You may seek spirit guides to aid you in your journey and help you with your intention. The travel is done by imagining the journey. Your imagination doesn't need to be vivid for it to work.

Find an environment where you could remain undisturbed for 30 minutes to an hour or so. This place should be safe, private, and free from distractions. The place is ideally dark; you will focus on internal images so it will help if your eyes are not distracted by what you see around you. You may light incense and candles that help you relax if you wish.

Be in the most comfortable position that you could get; one that won't restrict your breathing. You may sit, stand, or lie down if you prefer. Breathe deeply and easily. Close your eyes or cover them with a blindfold or eye mask. The researcher Michael Harner described a shamanic pose for journeying – lie on your back with outstretched legs. Position your right arm by your side with the fingers extended. Bend your left arm and place it over your eyes.

If it helps you focus more, you may chant, sing or pray. You may listen to shamanic drumming or a guided meditation recording.

Some have preparatory exercises before they do the shamanic journey. This may come in the form of meditative exercises, yoga, breathwork (e.g. Pranayama), or sacred rituals. You don't have to do them but they may help you enter a deeper trance.

Focus on an intention. Intention is important so you don't get lost in your journey. Having an intention will let the spirits help you better and prevent you from being distracted. Firmly announce your intention in your mind. You may also say this vocally. Shamans sometimes chant their intention repeatedly.

Again, focus on the sounds and the feeling of your breathing (or to the drumbeats if you are listening to them). Instruct your body to release tension, starting from the crown of your head all the way down to your toes. Allow relaxation to spread across your entire body.

When thoughts intrude your awareness, simply let them pass like clouds on the horizon. Do not fight against the thoughts because doing so will make them stick longer. Refocus on your breathing instead.

You will probably feel more sensations the deeper you sink into relaxation. You may feel tingling and hear buzzing in your ears. When you have completely relaxed, you may notice that your heart will beat faster and you may feel some vibrations. Don't be concerned with these because these will soon pass. Avoid becoming excited to prevent losing your trance.

At this point, you may perceive non-physical things around you – this is a sign that you are already journeying. If not, you may visualize a rope dangling above you. Reach out for this rope using your spirit hands (not your physical hands) and imagine climbing it. This will make you enter the energy realm of the Middle World. You may explore this place or go to the Lower or Upper Worlds.

It's always recommended to journey under the supervision of a reputable Shaman. Consider practicing with others in a group such us in Shamanic Workshops. IF you become exhausted, experience troubling symptoms, have difficult encounters in the Spirit Realms, or become disconnected from ordinary reality, refrain from journeying for the meantime until you find someone to guide you.

Ending a Journey

Shamanic journeys have to end at one point. If you are guided by drums, you will hear the drumming become faster and louder, or you may hear four distinct raps on the drum. This is the "callback" and it is the signal for preparing to finish your journey. When you hear this, hurry up with what you're doing. Thank your spirit guides and say your goodbyes.

The change of drumming may cause your state of mind to normalize. Your environment may fade or dissolve, or you may feel that you are moving away from the space.

You may also choose to come back even if you are not listening to drums or before the callback has been sounded. You can return when you've accomplished your intention, when your guides instructed you to wake up, or when you feel that you must end the journey. Announce to your guides that you have to come back to your ordinary reality.

Allow yourself to drift back gently into your physical body. You don't have to retrace your steps because your awareness is already anchored into the Middle World and it will return to it on its own. You just have to let go of your hold on the realm that you are in. You may also imagine something that belongs to the physical world, or just say aloud or in your mind that you want to come back now.

When your awareness comes back to the physical universe, try not to move suddenly to avoid becoming disoriented or straining your muscles. Reconnect with your body. See your spirit body merging with your flesh. Open your eyes gently and slowly. If there are any bright light sources nearby, look away from it to avoid hurting your eyes. Stretch your body and make gentle movements with your limbs.

If you haven't done so yet, write down everything you can remember from the journey. Write freely and don't try to censor or organize your thoughts – the more you do this, the more likely that you will forget details. Your task is to gather as much as you could from the journey; you can sort out the information later on a separate page of your notebook. Recording this way allows you to evaluate what happened, reflect on the lessons, uncover some answers, and integrate what you learned into your daily life.

Shamanic Journey Precautions

Shamanic journeying can bring benefits to your life if practiced carefully and wisely. However, there are some dangers to it.

For instance, repressed energies can come up to the surface of your awareness. Traumatic memories, hidden emotions, and destructive forces can manifest themselves more freely.

You must beware of spirits that masquerade as helpful guides but are in fact deceitful or malevolent entities. Your shadow self is one of these – it is your self-destructive aspect, and it may prevent you from being successful during your journeys.

Genuine spirit helpers will not force you into anything; they would simply advice you in what to do. They will not make you do anything dangerous to yourself or anyone else.

Journeying is only suitable for individuals who are psychologically healthy and socially and emotionally balanced. Do not attempt to go into the journeying process when you are severely stressed because whatever you encounter may only be a reflection of your troubled state. Remember that in the inner planes, whatever you think about often takes a life of their own, so if something bad is preoccupying you, you may find them magnified in the other realms. This is also the main reason why shamanic journeying must be accompanied by the calmest attitude possible.

Although it may help solve problems, shamanic journeys are not a recommended way to simply de-stress yourself. It is useful for accessing deep resources and guidance from conscious entities. You must be in your best state of mind; if you are exhausted and confused, you will become more vulnerable to malicious spirits and you may just get lost in self-generated illusions. Benevolent spirits may try to help you, but if your mind is clouded, you may not hear them properly.

As was mentioned earlier, shamanic journeying is not a de-stressing therapy because it involves accessing powerful subconscious resources and communicating with real, conscious beings. There are other ways to de-stress that are safer and more practical:

If you are already calm, you may listen to shamanic drumming to deepen your relaxation.

Grounding

Genuine traditional shamans use hallucinogens to aid their journeys, but they often live in close connection to nature. They are grounded and physically active, thus, their spiritual activities are balanced by their earthly existence. In comparison, modern humans living in cities are often disconnected from Mother Nature. They often have minds that are overstimulated by technology and intellectual pursuits. Because shamanic journeys and other practices may be too stimulating for you and create imbalance to your life, you are more vulnerable to this if you don't have an active lifestyle, spend too much time using gadgets, or have a desk job that involves a lot of thinking.

Because of this, you must find some way to ground yourself and connect your shamanic experiences with your everyday life. Aside from keeping yourself sane, grounding enables your life to actually improve. Going into these realms alone is not likely to create any obvious change in your life; after all, the shamans themselves go to the other worlds to gain guidance about what to do, and they re-enter this reality to implement them here.

Expecting the spirits to fix things for you is a form of dependency; it will prevent you from achieving real progress and it might be a turnoff to helper spirits. Remember that they observe what you do with what they give you. If they notice that you aren't using your shamanic knowledge for good, they might stop appearing to you. Remember that you are not a puppet of the spirit world but a co-creator of reality. If you want something, make it happen; nobody and nothing else is going to do it for you.

How to Ground Your Shamanic Journeys

There are some things you can do to ground your shamanic experiences to your reality. One way is by sharing them with other people, especially those who understand shamanism and have done journeys themselves. You may clothe them into a physical form by painting them, illustrating them, or making sculptures out of them. To make them more physical, use natural materials. To enable reflection, write about your experiences. You may convert it into a short story or poem. Surround yourself with pictures or objects which reflect the beings/power animals you meet

Real Vs Imagined

Imagination has always been equated to illusion, but it doesn't mean that shamanic journeys are only made up just because they happen in your mind. Imagination simply enables your mind to tune in to the reality of the other realms. It serves as the bridge between your awareness and the parallel dimensions. You can of course imagine things that are not real – you create them in another plane of existence, and it that plane, they exist, but practically speaking, they do not exist in the physical world. Even though they may be imaginary, they may still matter to you and those who encounter them if ever they manage to access where they are contained.

There is a difference between self-created imagination and non-physical realms, though. This is how to tell the difference. If you can still control what you're seeing or perceiving, it's likely that you are making it up. However, if you try to imagine a scene that's different from where you currently are, but it still remains, or if you manage to change it but it reverts to the same image, then it is likely to be real. When you become better at shamanic journeying, you will have scenes that are consistent.

Shamanic Journeying may be challenging for those who are new to the spirit realms. Fortunately, spirits can help you travel and do other tasks. Chapter 5 is about helpful spirits and how to acquire them.

Chapter 5. Helping Spirits

Helping spirits or spirit guides are non-physical beings that can protect, teach, heal, or help a person achieve certain goals that contribute to his/her spiritual development.

There are numerous types of guides – *souls of previous humans, ascended masters, angels, nature spirits, elementals, extraterrestrials, and even archetypes*. They can serve as guides for a short period of time or for life.

These guides may have previous incarnations before but have developed to the point that they no longer have to be incarnated again. Thus, they are free to help other beings evolve.

Guardian angels are also considered as spirit guides. These are said to not be an expression of God's power and have never been humans or other creatures before.

Pagans and shamans believe that an individual may have an animal spirit guide called an animal totem or power animal.

According to shamanic belief, each person is born with the spirit of one or more animals that guide him/her during life. Christianity also has a similar belief in guardian angel. Unlike guardian angels though, a person is said to lose and gain some spirit animals depending on their needs, what happens to them or what they do.

Ancestral Guides are acquired through family lineage and only accompanies an individual on important occasions. They may be deceased family members or ancient ancestors.

Ascended Masters are beings who are highly evolved spiritually. They have already overcome their karma and have managed to reunite with the divine.

Elementals are linked to the four elements of Earth, Fire, Air, and Water and they gain their abilities and strengths from them. They can be mischievous but can also offer good qualities like persistence and stability (earth), intelligence and flexibility (air), courage and will (fire), and empathy and calmness (water).

Communicating With Spirit Guides

Conversing with spirits can be tricky. You must know whether you are talking to a genuine being or just your own imagination. For this, you must always check whether something in your mind is making up the experience.

Talking with spirit helpers is like talking with a person who knows you well. You can't really lie to spirits since your mind is an open book to them. Sometimes, you don't have to say anything, but they will already know what you need to hear from them. If you want their cooperation, it's important that you are honest with them and you don't try to manipulate them in any way. You may of course try to exert your will over them but there will be consequences for that.

Although spirits can manifest themselves to non-believers, it's helpful if you believe in their existence. Disbelief may cause your mind to filter out their manifestations or explain them away as something else. You may increase your faith in spirits and spirit guides by researching more about them and talking to those who work with them regularly.

Spirit messages may come in various forms – they may not come in words of your native language but as ideas, pictures, symbols, scents, moods, sensations, memories, coincidences, and more. You may perceive their communication in your own mind, from the environment, or from an overlap of both.

Guides can come to you without you seeking for them, but you may also reach out to them when you need something whether it may be emotional support, companionship, protection, guidance, or healing.

You can meet guides in the spirit realm through the vehicle of your own mind. For this, you must turn your awareness inwards and away from the external physical world.

Eliminate your distractions and empty your mind of preoccupations. When you have reached an altered state of consciousness, create an imaginary space where you and the guide can meet and converse with each other.

This space should feel safe for you. You may enclose the place with a barrier such as a gate, a fence, a wall, a row of trees – anything that will set it apart from the rest of the terrain. Instruct this barrier to protect you from all harm. Put a passageway somewhere on this barrier. This is where the guides can enter or leave your space. Instruct this gateway to let in only good spirits and beneficial energies.

Imagine being in this place and ask for your spirit guide to come to you. If you have a particular spirit guide in mind, you may mention its name. You may also request someone who has particular traits to appear. Or, you may just state your intention and ask if someone is interested to be your guide for it. Maintain a passive attitude and just wait until someone arrives or something happens.

Expect that someone or something will appear at the entrance. Pretend that someone is already waiting outside and open the door.

Pay close attention to your experiences. How does your guide manifest itself? Does anything about your guide's presence, appearance, or movement strike you? Can you tell whether your guide is male or female? Can you smell perfume? Notice as much as you can.

Begin a conversation if the guide hasn't communicated yet. Introduce yourself then ask what the guide's name is. You may ask why it has come to you and whether it has a message for you. You may ask your guide anything you want but you must not force it to respond in particular ways. It will tell you what it wants you to know and what you need to know. If you force the guide to give you answers that you want to hear, your imagination may fabricate the conversation.

When you feel satisfied or when you have to leave, tell your guide that you have to go. Thank the guide for talking to you. Before leaving, you may ask how you may recognize the guide and how it wants to be called.

Power Animals – What Are They?

Your Power Animal will not be something you are afraid of or are repulsed by. It is something you can love and be comfortable with. Do not accept animal that bares its teeth at you or acts aggressively. You must keep in mind that the spirits you encounter may attempt to communicate with you. Don't mistake aggressiveness as a sign that the animal is boasting about its power so that it will be accepted as a guide. You must respect its wishes and avoid taking guides with you without their consent. They may retaliate; worse, they may tell other spirit beings about your rudeness, and if they do, you might lose your opportunity to communicate with these other entities.

Learn about spirit animals not only in your shamanic journeys, but also by watching physical animals in nature. This will increase trust between you and the spirit animals and enhance your ability to communicate with them.

If you can't find one in your shamanic journeys, think about the animal that you are most drawn to. What creature/s do you feel the most connected with? Are you interested in learning all about a particular animal? If you're in nature, what animal/s do you notice most? Does a specific animal show up in your dreams often? Do creatures enter your mind as you meditate, pray, or reflect?

Animals may include not only furry creatures but also amphibians, reptiles, birds, and insects.

Your Power Animal is not an ordinary animal spirit; it is your constant guide and companion. Power Animals are usually obtained from the Lower World because that's their natural habitat, but you may also find some in the Middle and Upper Worlds.

Take note that it's more likely that you will find spirit guides in both the Upper World, and if you got a Power Animal from the Middle World, it may not be as powerful and wise as compared to those from the Lower World. Keep in mind that the spirit of a living or deceased pet may show itself in your journeys and help you out, but they are considered as familiars and not Power Animals. The latter are usually Oversouls of an entire species while pets are individual souls.

Finding Your Power Animal

Go to the Lower World and search for a safe clearing. Ask for your Power Animal to appear. Wait quietly and observe.

- The response may come when an animal shows itself, or when you see parts of the animal flashing in front of your eyes such as its eyes, beak, feathers, and wings. You may also hear the sound of an animal or otherwise feel the essence of it.

- Let go of your preferences and expectations and watch what actually approaches you. Is there an animal that is constantly following you?

- Ask if it is your Power Animal. It may say yes or no or give a signal for this. For example, hugging or licking you may mean yes, while baring its teeth or running away may mean no.

- Again, the animal will send signals to tell you if it is your guide. You just have to sharpen your senses to get them. Sometimes you will just know that it is your guide. There will be recognition between both of you that surpass words.

- If the Power Animal doesn't show itself the first time you called, keep trying. One will eventually come to you.

- When you found it, stay with it even if other animals or being show up. You may ride your Power Animal or shapeshift into its body. You may also ask it for healing and guidance. If the journey stops moving, you can ask your Power Animal what to do next.

- Bring your Power Animal with you when you return. When you hear the drum callback, embrace the Power Animal and push it down into your heart. Feel it becoming one with your body.

Spirit guides and Power Animals are helpful with a lot of tasks such as healing yourself or someone else. Chapter 6 is about shamanic healing – how it is done and how you can perform a healing.

Chapter 6. Shamanic Healing

Healing is one of the major duties of a Shaman. As you've read earlier, what distinguishes a Shaman from a Medicine Man is his/her ability to effect healing by conversing with spirits and affecting the person's condition at the energetic level.

All illnesses, whether they may be caused by natural or supernatural things, has a spiritual component. This is what the shaman can search for and address when journeying for someone else. The illness may be the manifestation from negative emotions, soul loss, soul attachments, and the likes. For this, the shaman will find solutions and heal the target while in the Spirit Realms. The shaman returns and shares the information he/she has obtained to the client. After this, it is the client's own responsibility to complete his/her healing process.

Shamans can obtain wisdom from the spirit realms and pass it on to other people. They can manipulate energy and use it for healing purposes. The actual healing takes place within the patient's spirit, so it is up to him/her whether he/she accepts this healing, and he must be responsible for his/her healing process.

Remember that shamanic healing must not replace psychological and medical interventions.

They may only be used to complement these kinds of healing.

The Spirits can help diagnose the cause of the illness and perform the healing. They can also suggest what people could do to help the person.

The healing could take place indoors or outdoors in a sacred space conducive to healing – in other words, it is safe, quiet, comfortable, relaxing, and equipped with the materials that can aid the patient's wellbeing.

It can contain an altar and decorated with shamanic instruments, crystals, incenses, candles, and the like. Soft meditative or shamanic music may be played in the background.

Before the healing session, there is an open conversation between the patient and the shaman. The shaman learns the client's history – his/her medical conditions, health status, psychological issues, life experiences, and other information that can uncover the nature of the problem. The shaman also learns about how the patient's soul is doing.

The Shaman will assess the patient's various energy centers. He/she will determine whether there are stagnant, blocked, or excessive energy. He/she will then manipulate these energies to restore energetic balance. The patient may experience tingling or warming sensations as his/her energy is manipulated. Aside from that, the patient may release energy in the form of emotional outbursts or surfacing memories.

The Shaman may go on a journey to channel guidance and energy from the spirit world. He/she can move through the client's body in spirit form. To prevent the illness from going back, the Shaman may fill the patient's with power so the negative entity or spirit can't stay in it. This can take an hour to accomplish

When the Shaman returns, he/she discusses what he/she has experienced in the spirit realms. Shaman and patient will discuss what can be done.

The shamanic intervention must then be integrated into the client's life. This process may take days to months. The client takes note of what he/she experiences and the things he/she does; these may be written in a journal to keep track of progress.

Since energetic toxins are released and energy is shifted, the client may experience discomfort and changes in his/her life. Although these may be troublesome, they are a normal part of the healing process. For this, the shaman frequently checks with the client to help him/her overcome these difficulties.

Causes of Illnesses

Shamans treat these energetic causes of illnesses:

- <u>Power Loss</u>

Power loss is caused by the person's disconnection to his/her source of power. This may happen when he/she has experienced something that has caused him/her to lose sight of life's meaning. Rejecting the existence of help of spirit guides may cause this, as well as misusing one's own energy. The loss of life power and will creates chaos on the person's energetic matrix, which causes him/her to be more vulnerable to illness. He/she may develop anxieties, be prone to distractions, and become aimless.

A shaman solves this by journeying the shamanic realms and reconnecting the disempowered person to sources of power such as Power Animals and Spirit Guides. The shaman may gather energy from the realms and transfer it to the person. He/she may instruct the client to acknowledge the presence of his/her Guides and seek their help whenever necessary.

- <u>Negative Emotions</u>

Negative emotions such as fear, anger, and sadness may cause energetic imbalances. The shaman will find the root causes of these emotions, converse with them to know what the issue is, and carry out interventions. He/she will advise the patient on what to do to reduce negative feelings and encourage positive ones.

- <u>Stagnant or Sluggish Flow of Energy</u>

The quality and flow of energy in the person's energy field affects the state of his physical and psychological health. Illnesses may result when the energy flow becomes stagnant or sluggish. This unnatural motion may be caused by unhealthy behaviors, stress, or internal conflict. The Shaman helps the client become aware of these causes so that the energy will be reactivated.

- <u>Energy Blockages</u>

The prolonged pooling of sluggish energy may develop into energy blockages. These are caused by repressed thoughts and emotions, conditioning, trauma, abuse, self-destructive habits, addiction, and inflexibility. The patient may report feelings of being stuck or blocked.

These blockages are treated through intention and visualization. The Shaman will first ask the blockage what the Shaman needs to know. The Shaman and the patient can then visualize the blockage being removed. They can imagine that it is being eaten up, destroyed, or opening up.

Intrusions are energy forms that are more solid than usual. The Shaman may resort to extraction for these. These stubborn energy forms may be caused by localized trauma, psychic attacks, intense negative thoughts and emotions, old issues, energetic imprints, and discarnate entities. These can cause discomfort, pain, and strong unpleasant emotions. The Shaman pulls this out using shamanic or energetic tools.

Dismemberment happens to shamans, but a shaman may also dismember a patient as a drastic measure to remove illnesses, blockages, and intrusions. Only the soul of the patient is dismembered while the body doesn't feel any pain because of the procedure. It is reassembled into a newer, healthier form.

- <u>Energy Leakages</u>

The patient's energy field may be punctured because of attacks or self-generated negativity resulting from a problem, habit, or circumstance. This causes energy leaks. This is a problem because an energy field with holes is in risk of being invaded by unwanted forces. The Shaman scans the energy field to see where it leaks. He/she visualizes its healings – for instance, he/she can imagine it closing up like a healing wound. He/she can also use tools to knit or weave the torn edges together.

- <u>Energetic Cords</u>

Cords represent unhealthy attachments between two or more individuals. The Shaman inspects the cord and gathers information from it. He/she then removes the cord by pulling it from where it is connected to the person and the other/s. He/she may also visualize cutting the cord using a sharp tool. To heal the space left by the cord, the Shaman fills it up with healing energies.

- <u>Entities</u>

Discarnate entities may attach themselves to someone because they want to experience having a body or because they are attracted to the person in some way. They may also be sent by a sorcerer to spy on the person or to make his/her life miserable. People who have entities may experience personality or behavioral changes, not seem to be in their usual selves, or become ill because of unexplainable reasons.

If this is the case, the shaman will de-possess the client. He/she will talk with the entity and know why it is there. Depending on the case or on the methods of the shaman, the entity may be helped, escorted out or forcefully evicted.

- <u>Hauntings</u>

Spirits of the deceased can get trapped in the middle world because they are unaware of having died, scared of crossing over, or refuse to leave because of attachments or unfinished business. The shaman will listen to the ghosts and assist it to leave. He/she will gather the spirit's energy and remove it from the premises.

- <u>Soul Loss</u>

Soul loss happens when a person becomes so threatened that a portion of his/her soul breaks off and hide in a safe place in the spirit realms. This is just a coping mechanism; when the danger passes, this soul fragment returns to the person if he/she is ready to accept it. There are times though when the person can't receive the soul parts yet, thus, he/she becomes weak, confused, and unable to cope with life.

Soul Loss may manifest itself through the following:

- A feeling of being incomplete or broken
- Inaccessible memories
- Lack of motivation
- Apathy
- Depression
- Suicidal tendencies
- Overall negativity

When this happens, soul retrieval may be necessary. The Shaman journeys through all the worlds to find the missing soul fragments and returns them to the owner. He/she gathers the energies in his/her hands, heart, or a sacred vessel before transferring them to the client. He/she may also blow this to the client's energy field. When the soul fragment is returned, the shaman seals the energy field and fortifies it using a rattle.

- <u>Vulnerable Soul Parts</u>

Just as Shamans can restore soul fragments, they can also separate a piece of the person's soul. This is done to protect it from harm or stolen – especially when it contains something desirable. The Shaman will take this part and hide it somewhere safe, and during its stay there, it will gain in strength. The Shaman may do this to his/her own soul to make it grow stronger.

Performing a Simple Shamanic Healing

Healing must be done with the person's permission, or else the energies that will be sent may be unwelcome so it won't have any effect. Worse, it may be perceived as an attack so the person may fight against it. You must ask permission even if you think that the person needs your help or that he/she doesn't have to know what you're doing. You may be able to do it and it may have intended effects, but this will leave an impression on the spirits.

Sometimes, people become ill because they want to be sick, or at least, a part of them does. To avoid hassle, you must ask if they really want to be healed.

Like with a shamanic journey, prepare your blindfold, shamanic drumming music, and pen and paper at ready. Play the drumming, put on a blindfold, and go to the Axis Mundi. Upon reaching it, tell the Power Animal about who you are trying to heal and what needs to be healed.

Go down to the Lower World with the Power Animal with the intention of finding the person in the Lower World so you could heal them. You simply have to tell the Power Animal this and then you follow where they go. The Power Animal will know what to do and where to find the person.

You may find yourself in a place you've not been before, but this is the one that's suitable for your healing target. The problem may be apparent to you when you see the person, or you may not notice anything different. You don't need to know what you should do to heal the person; you just have to ask the Power Animal to do the healing. Just watch what it does and learn what you could.

Other animals or shamans may come and help; if they do, ask the Power Animal if they can participate. They should be trustworthy enough.

When events slow down or stop before the drumming does, ask the Power Animal what else must be done – this will cause things to happen again. When you hear the drum call-back signal, return to your physical body fully. Ask your Power Animal to cleanse and disentangle you from the client. Afterwards, tell what happened to the person while they take down notes. Instruct the client to reflect on what happened.

Shamanic healing may be done on the spirit realms, but it can also be done during dreams. The next chapter is about using dreams for shamanic work.

Chapter 7. Dreamwork

Dreams are a form of altered state of consciousness. In dreaming, you can access your own subconscious mind as well as the different worlds of the axis mundi. Because of this, making the most of your dreams will make you a better shaman.

These dreams may also be a form of communication between one's own soul and that of others. Your guides and your own subconscious mind may send information, advice and warnings to you in your dream. On the other hand, lost souls and spirit intrusions may also affect what you dream about. Nightmares of suffering and dying may be memories of souls that have attached to a dreaming person; these should not be confused as one's own past life memories. If there are recurring strange dreams, a shaman will trace the origin of the dream and do the necessary interventions.

Power-filled people are said to be protected from dreams caused by intrusions and unhelpful spirits. If you suspect that some dreams or nightmares have a supernatural cause, you may seek the help of a shaman. You may also heal yourself.

Lucid dreaming is being aware that you are in a dream and controlling what happens in that dream. In the dreamscape, you can find the meaning of your previous dreams, find the solutions to predicaments, work through issues, promote healing, talk with spirits, and so on. This is similar to regular shamanic journeying but you will enter a deeper state of mind, which will enable more genuine experiences.

There are guided meditations, lucid dreaming apps, and equipment that will help you dream lucidly. These may help, but it's still better if you learn to do it without relying on external tools. These are some techniques to help you with that.

As you are falling asleep, imagine doing something. Pretend that you are making the movements with your body. This will keep your mind active enough to maintain awareness as you enter a dream.

Ask yourself if you are dreaming or awake every time you do or experience a particular thing, such as when you pass through a doorway, drink a glass of water, or sneeze. There may be a time when this will happen in a dream; the habit of asking may lead you to realize that you are dreaming, and this makes you control the dream.

During the day, immerse yourself in things that are related to the kind of dream you want to have. Look at pictures or draw what you want to happen. Describe to yourself what you plan to dream about. Remind yourself that you must remember that you are dreaming when you find yourself in that dream.

Make it a daily habit to record your dreams in a dream diary. This trains your mind into paying attention to what you dream about to the point that you will be alert while in a dreaming state. Aside from this, you will spot some dream signs, or occurrences that are common in your dreams. Examples of these signs are the following:

- Finding yourself in unusual places
- Objects, creatures, places and people look different and behave in strange ways
- You see people around you who are dead or somewhere far away
- You can do impossible things like fly in the air or walk through a wall

Choose a dream sign and tell yourself that you will realize that you are dreaming when you encounter them. For example: "I will know that I am dreaming whenever I float to the sky."

A non-lucid dream may lead to a lucid dream, but you may also head straight into one. You can do this by forcing yourself to dream by closing your eyes, lying still, and waiting for sleep to come to you. Wait until you see hallucinations in front of your closed eyelids. The images will become more and more complex until you enter a dream scene.

If you find it difficult to go straight into a dream from waking, you may sleep normally and wake yourself after six hours with the help of an alarm clock. When you wake up, go out of bed and do something for 20 minutes. Return to your bed and imagine what you want to dream. Because you have stimulated your mind, it's possible that your dream self will wake up in the middle of a dream.

You may control the dream by:

- Changing the images until they form the things you want to see
- Announcing what you want to happen
- Willing it to form

If what you are forming doesn't show up, look away for a moment and look back. It's likely that it will appear in front of you.

If you want to change the dream, simply spin around.

If you find the dream environment dissolving, or if you feel your awareness slipping away, lie down in the dream. It will make the dream persist.

If you want to wake up, just tell yourself that you want to wake up. You will find yourself awake a few moments later.

If you are having a bad dream, you can change the dream into something more pleasant or even funny. Relax and think about something that makes you happy. Your mood will affect the content of your dream.

Incubating dreams

Decide what you will dream about. You may want to get the solution to a problem, an answer to a question, or ideas for something you are working on. Write down your intention or question on paper.

Read this again and again within the day and before you sleep.

When you're in bed, read it and ask your dreaming mind to bring you what you requested during sleep. You may put the paper near your bed or underneath your pillow.

Declare what you want to happen. "I will have a dream that (insert your goal here). As I wake up, I will remember this dream, write it down, and know what it means."

Relax your body and mind as you sleep. When you wake up, remember everything you can and write them down immediately. Just write things as they arrive; you can organize them later. Do this without going up from your bed as much as possible – if you get up already and moved a lot, your brain may be prompted to activate your wakeful mode, and this will erase whatever you dreamed about.

Shifting Your Perspective

This exercise trains you to shift your perspective into someone else's. This will help with shapeshifting to a Power Animal as well.

Choose a dream that's still fresh in your memory. A good dream to choose is something that is almost as convincing as what you are experiencing right now while you're awake. This dream should be something that involves 3D space instead of being abstract or story-like. It should also contain dream characters aside from yourself, whether they are humans, animals, or other beings.

Find a place where you can remain undisturbed for about 30 minutes. Lie on your back or sit in a meditative pose on a chair or on the floor. Read the instructions first and remember them before doing what they say. You can also record the steps and play them later on.

Close your eyes. Relax yourself until you enter the state between waking and sleeping. Be aware of your breathing and count from twenty to ten. Imagine taking a step down the stars as you count. When you go down, feel yourself sink deeper towards sleep. Upon reaching ten, stop and feel the state of consciousness you're in, and notice whether it's different from the first moment when you began counting.

It doesn't really matter whether you notice the difference or not; what's important is that you realize that your state of consciousness shifts, such as what happens when you reflect upon your state. Afterwards, count from ten to zero and sink even deeper. You will come close to sleeping but hover above that level.

Count from ten to zero once more. Feel your awareness sink from the top your head, on your face, through your neck, torso, arms, legs, and down to your feet. Notice what you experience as you do this. When your awareness is within your feet, enter the dream you have selected.

Position yourself in the dream place where your dream-self was before. Look around. Is the area light or dark? Is this a large space or small? Are you on a high or low elevation? What do you see in front of you? How about when you turn to the right, left, or behind? Focus on a single object and estimate your distance from it. Is it big or tiny? What are its color, shape, and texture? Turn wherever you want but do it slowly. Observe as many items as you can. Be aware of any sounds, smells, and sensations too. Is there a floor or a ground underneath your feet? Is there a sky or roof above you? What is the mood in there – lively, gloomy, terrifying, or boring?

Look for another being in the area within the dream. When you find one, estimate how far away you are from this person or creature. How do you feel about it? What do you expect it would feel about you? Observe this individual closely – how does it look like? What does its facial expressions and body language express? Imagine how this other being feels. Copy its posture or movements. How does it feel? Do this until you begin to empathize with him/her. Slowly enter this person's point of view – you can enter by looking deep into its eyes or copying its posture and motions. Wait until you feel how it's like to be this other being.

Observe the space from the other's viewpoint. Look around. How does this being see the area? This may experience the environment differently than you. As this other being, locate your dream self. Look at this dream self. What does this self look like from its perspective? Stay with this experience for as long as you could. If there are other individuals in the dream, try the process with them too, but do these very slowly.

When you get tired or if you lose your dream images, or if you feel that you've already done just enough, prepare to return to your normal awareness. Count slowly from one to twenty. Notice how your consciousness expands as it moves back to the surface. Observe too how your environment changes.

Avoid being too tried before sleeping because this may cause you to fail becoming lucid in dreams.

Interpreting Dreams

You will find many lists of dream interpretations. These may help you somewhat, but they are only generic meanings and they may or may not apply to your situation. It's better if you interact with the dream to know it more intimately. You may ask it questions like these:

- Can you explain to me why I had that dream?
- Are you showing me my desires/fears/preoccupations?
- Are you telling me that I should do something?
- Are you giving me advice?
- Are you warning me of something?

This is best done as soon as you wake up when the dream is still fresh in your mind. If some time has passed, do this at a time when you can clear your mind of preoccupations.

Another way to know the meaning of dreams is through free association. Replay the dream or the parts of it that you want to understand. What thoughts come up? List them down.

You can ask helping spirits to help you interpret a dream. They may show you what has caused the dream as well.

Record your dreams and try to interpret them. Aside from having a dream diary, also have a journal where you record what happens during the day. When you compare your dreams with your daily experiences, you may understand why you have certain dreams and what they could mean. You may also spot some precognitive dreams.

So far, you have learned how to work with the spirits of guides and animals. The upcoming chapter is about working with plants like shamans do.

Chapter 8. Working with Plants

Warning: don't use psychoactive (mind-altering) plants if you don't know what you're doing. Some plants are highly toxic, and even if you used relatively harmless plants, you might die if they are prepared incorrectly or consumed in large doses. It's best if you take these plants under the guidance of a shaman with a lot of experience with the plant you want to use. There should also be assistants around who can help you in case you get into trouble – if you experience troublesome symptoms, they may give you an antidote, for example. Although many have tried psychoactive plants and survived, there are a few who didn't. Consume them at your own risk.

You may have read some stories about people who have taken substances and had life-changing, mind-boggling experiences as a result. Yes, they do happen; many have learned things they didn't know before and have overcome tough challenges with the help of plant teachers. It's likely that these people were also warned about the dangers, but their conviction to learn from the plant spirit won over their fear. Thus, you need to ask yourself: are you willing to undergo discomfort, terror, and possible death in exchange for the plant teacher's supernatural gifts?

If you answered yes, it's best that you make yourself as strong and resilient as possible, not only physically, but also psychologically and spiritually. However, if you have severe medical or psychiatric conditions, it's wise to be on the safe side and not take psychoactives.

You must consult your doctor and tell him/her about your plans of taking shamanic plants; you may or may not be given the go signal depending on your status and the plant's potential reactions to medications you are taking.

You don't need to consume psychoactives to travel the spirit realms and access inner resources, after all. You just have to enter an altered state of awareness, and as you have learned, this can be done through several safe ways.

With that being said, an important part of shamanism is working with plant spirits. Through thousands of years, shamans have interacted with nature and learned which plants are helpful to humans and which of them harmful. They discovered how to prepare them so they achieve desired effects such as opening their eyes to the unseen worlds.

Hallucinogens such as psychoactive plants are used for several reasons such as:

- To confront their repressed issues
- To understand themselves better
- To find solutions to tough problems

- To gain insights
- To perceive the world and themselves differently
- To explore the other dimensions
- To be aware of and interact with spirits and subtle energies

Some take hallucinogens simply to be entertained, but having a shallow intention may not lead to profound insights. In comparison, shamans treat psychoactive plants with respect. They use them to achieve important purposes that will benefit the community.

Shamans have used psychoactive plants for working with spiritual beings and forces. They ingest them to enter a realm where they could do things that are considered as impossible in the normal world, such as talk with nature spirits, contact departed souls, heal ailments on the energetic level, solve a problem under the direction of knowledgeable beings, find missing objects, uncover secrets, and more.

Since shamans believe that everything is conscious, alive, and intelligent, they perceive spirits in plants. To them, they can serve as teachers and healers while they are in a trance.

Before going into trance, the plants are prepared in particular ways that are said to please the spirit. The shaman and participants of their rituals also undergo preparations such as taking ritual baths and eating a specific diet.

The spirits of the plants are known to appear as humans, as animals, or a combination of both. How it manifests itself may depend on the occasion and the people who perceive them.

For instance, the spirit of Ayahuasca is seen as a mother, but it may show itself as a snake. The spirit of Uña de Gato Vine manifests itself as a strong man with claws, but sometimes as a jaguar.

The gender of the plant spirit may vary as well depending on whether masculine or feminine energy is needed for the healing. As an example, the Pucalupuna tree spirit displays itself as a cat-eyed woman and at other times as a man with multiple heads. However, some plant spirits have a consistent gender. Ayahuasca is perceived to be female while Iboga is observed to be male.

Sometimes, the spirit's appearance is connected to the plant's nature. The name of the Ayahuma tree translates to spirit head. When its fruit falls to the ground, it splits open. Eventually, the exposed pulp rots and releases a smell similar to rotting flesh. Thus, the Ayahuma tree reveals itself as a headless woman or a man with his head within his chest.

The Sangre de Grado tree's reddish sap is used for treating ailments such as ulcers, wounds, and infections. Its spirit is seen to be a man having a red body. The Remocaspi tree tends to appear as a doctor perhaps because of its medicinal properties. Hardwood tree spirits are reported to look like tall, powerful men.

Ingestion of psychoactive plants is usually done in a ceremony under the direction of a trained shaman. The shaman will then guide and protect those under his/her care. He/she helps the participants interpret and understand their experiences and integrate them later on in their lives.

Before participating in such a ceremony, the participants must be ready and willing to surrender to the plant spirit. They must not be forced into it because it is a serious matter. Because of its risks, only those who are fully committed to receive help from the plant spirit despite danger should participate in the ceremony.

Ayahuasca

Ayahuasca is one of the most popular among the teacher plants; its popularity has caused flocks of tourists to seek shamans and participate in ayahuasca rituals. Ayahuasca is illegal in almost all countries except Peru, Ecuador, Colombia, Bolivia, and Brazil. In these places, there are places where shamans can perform ayahuasca ceremonies to foreigners.

The Ayahuasca brew is composed of chacruna leaf and Ayahuasca vine – both of these plants thrive in the Amazon rainforest in South

America. It is prepared by the shaman and drank as a sacred tree in an enclosed ritual place. It is usually done at night time so that the participants can more easily see the visions that the brew will provoke.

One week prior to the ceremony, participants will prepare before the ceremony by taking an ayahuasca diet or dieta. They will abstain from processed food, junk food, alcohol, and drugs. Some diets also forbid the ingestion of meat, spices, salt, and sugar. This is to prepare the body and mind for the plant spirit.

Ayahuasca will cause purging – that is, the participants will defacate and vomit. This removes the toxins from the body and from the energy field. The dieta will decrease the severity of the purging.

The shaman stays at the center while the participants form a circle around him/her. The table containing the ayahuasca and other shamanic implements are placed in front of the shaman. The position of the people aims to concentrate the energy at the point where the table is.

Participants may sit upon chairs or on mats. Shamanic songs called Icaros are often sung to begin the ceremony and invite good spirits to come. The Shaman sings into the container of Ayahuasca then pours it into the participant's cups. He/she sings into each participant's cups as well.

When everyone has consumed the Ayahuasca tea, the lights and candles are turned off. The Icaros is sung again along with the shamanic drums and rattles. These sounds direct the energy flows to cleanse and protect the palace. They will also guide the participants in their journeys and bestow healing upon them.

The ceremony lasts somewhere from four to six hours. The effects may start from 20 minutes to one hour after drinking it. It's not advisable to drink more just because the effects are not yet felt; drinking too much may cause you to be overwhelmed. The experience will depend on the dosage of the brew and the ingredients used, as well as the drinker's metabolism and diet.

The participants must not ask to drink before the shaman hands over the cup to them. He/she will provide the drink at a time when the spirits direct him/her to or when he/she sense that the participant is ready.

When everyone has drunk the tea, they sit in the darkness and contemplate on what they experience. They should refrain from talking to each other so that they can fully concentrate on the messages of the plant spirit.

Participants should refrain from leaving the sacred space when under the influence of Ayahuasca. One reason for this is the brew may cause disorientation; another is that the participants are more sensitive to the unseen and are more attractive to wandering spirits.

Leaving the protected space may expose them to malevolent spirits and harmful energies.

The room will be lighted again before the ceremony closes. The shamans and participants may interact with each other at this moment and talk about what happened. Those who want to sleep may do so.

Eating meals are delayed until noon the following day. Eating food immediately after drinking Ayahuasca may cause vomiting.

Ayahuasca is just one of the numerous plants that are used for shamanic work. Again, you must be careful about the plants you consume and never do things without adequate research and preparation.

Plant Magic

Shamans use plants not only for healing and journeying; they use it for magic as well. They are different from herbalists because they also know the spiritual and magical uses of plants. There are many books about how you can use plants for shamanic and magical work; the plants and the procedures that are discussed will vary depending on the tradition.

People believe that plants are effective in magic because of the forces that underlie and connect everything in existence; in certain kinds of plants, there are forces that are conducive to achieving particular effects such as increasing prosperity, instilling hope, banishing negativities, and the like. Using these plants with the intention of releasing their potentials into our reality may indeed cause those things to manifest.

Like what shamans discovered, certain plants have powerful spirits in them. They contain their own intelligence so they can help a person achieve what he/she desires. However, when a person contacts these spirits, he/she must make sure that the spirit is genuinely helpful or it may grant his/her wishes in mischievous ways. The person and the spirit must also communicate well to prevent misunderstandings and wrong results.

When using plants for magic, the shaman may charge the plants with energy from the spirit realms. The energy he/she uses is harmonized to his/her intention. He/she chooses the appropriate plants and items since each thing in existence has its own energy signature that resonates with particular intentions and not others.

Cleansing the Items

Plants and other items used in the ritual are ideally cleansed to eliminate unwanted energies that may interfere with the magical work. This is essential when other people have come into contact with these items, since their energies and thoughtforms may become attached to the items.

Ritual objects may be cleansed by rinsing it with water, passing them through incense smoke, ringing a bell or shaking a rattle over them, or visualizing negative energies being drained from them. You may also ask the help of your spirit guides and power animals for cleansing.

After cleansing, you must keep them in a place where other people will not touch them to prevent them from contaminating the items with their energies.

Charging

Plants and items in nature have energy, but you will amplify and guide the energy better if you charge them prior to casting your spell. When they are charged, you can use these items to contain the energy or release it to the universe.

Some ways for charging items are the following:

- Hold the items with your dominant hand. The hand that you use more frequently is said to release energy more strongly than your other hand. Visualize your entire body glowing with pure energy. In your mind's eye, let this energy pool upon the palm of your hand and seep into your items.

- Put your items on top of some crystals. You may also surround your items with crystals. Natural crystals are formed for thousands to millions of years and thus contain stored energy. You may program the crystals to lend their energy to your items. Simply tell the crystals what it should do. You could also visualize energy flowing out of the crystals and into your items. For maximum effect, leave the items with the crystals for an entire day.

- Let the items soak moonlight. Moonlight is believed to contain magical energy, while sunlight has more of a physical energy. Remove these items before sunrise to prevent it from flushing out the subtle energy that has accumulated in the objects.

- Light candles with the color that remind you of your intention – for example, green candles may be used for healing, yellow for gaining clarity, and red for igniting passion. Place your items in a container near the candle. Imagine the light and color of the candle pooling into the container where your items are.

You may stop charging your items when you feel they are already loaded with energy. You can sense this as warmth, a breeze, or a tingling when you put your hand near the items. You may also catch some bright sparkles or transparent waves from them. Otherwise, you may just have the gut feeling that they're ready.

The Ritual

Although magical rituals can seem complex, they are simply representations of what you want to happen. What's important is that you focus on your intention, visualize the results, and put energy into it so that it can manifest in the physical world. You can find a lot of magical rituals around; you may experiment with them and create some of your own using your shamanic abilities. To achieve the best results, work with your spirit guides, and never forget to do something in your physical reality to bring yourself closer to your goal.

Conclusion

You have just learned shamanic secrets that other people may not be aware of. Would you use this to dominate others? Or would you use your shamanic knowledge for the betterment of humans? The Spirits are kind; they allow people to do what they want, but they are also kind enough to let them face the consequences of what they do so they can learn from it.

Shamanic learning can never be completed by simply reading a book. As what was suggested earlier, it's better if you find a shaman who could teach you his/her craft. Spend time with people who have experience with shamanic work so you will know how to do it properly.

Never forget that as a shaman, your main teachers are the Spirits. You must keep your shamanic eyes open to their reality, but at the same time, you must keep your feet grounded to this reality so your learnings will be of value to the world.

Don't allow your education to remain on the intellectual level; do the exercises, perform the activities. There are those who are content with reading other people's experiences. You will never be a shaman if you stay on the surface.

Always remember that the Spirit cares about you. It wants to give you good things and protect you from the bad. You don't have to be afraid of what you will encounter in the spirit realms for as long as you keep yourself safe in the physical. Explore as much as you could and bring valuable stuff back. Doing this makes you a true shaman of the modern age.

Made in the USA
Middletown, DE
12 December 2018